The Wayland Library of Science and Technology

THE SCIENCE OF LIFE

CLINT TWIST

The Wayland Library of Science and Technology

The Nature of Matter
The Universal Forces
Stars and Galaxies
The Solar System
The Changing Landscape
Air and Oceans
Origins of Life
The Science of Life
Plants and Animals
Animal Behaviour
The Human Machine
Health and Medicine

The Environment
Feeding the World
Raw Materials
Manufacturing Industry
Energy Sources
The Power Generators
Transport
Space Travel
Communications
The Computer Age
Scientific Instruments
Towards Tomorrow

Advisory Series Editor
Robin Kerrod

Consultants
Professor D.C. Imrie, Dr P. Whitfield

Editor: Steve Luck
Designer: David West · Children's Book Design
Production: Steve Elliott
Art Director: John Ridgeway
Project Director: Lawrence Clarke

First published in 1990 by
Wayland (Publishers) Ltd
61 Western Road, Hove
East Sussex BN3 1JD, England

AN EQUINOX BOOK

Planned and produced by:
Equinox (Oxford) Limited
Musterlin House, Jordan Hill Road,
Oxford OX2 8DP

Copyright © Equinox (Oxford) Ltd 1990

British Library Cataloguing in Publication Data
Twist, Clint
The Science of Life
1. Organisms
I. Title
574

ISBN 1-85210-892-4

Media conversion and typesetting by Peter
MacDonald, Una Macnamara and Vanessa Hersey
Origination by Hong Kong Reprohouse Co Ltd
Printed in Italy by Rotolito Lombarda
S.p.A., Milan
Bound in France by AGM

Front cover: Nerve cells growing in
tissue culture in a laboratory.
Back cover: The process called photosynthesis.

Contents

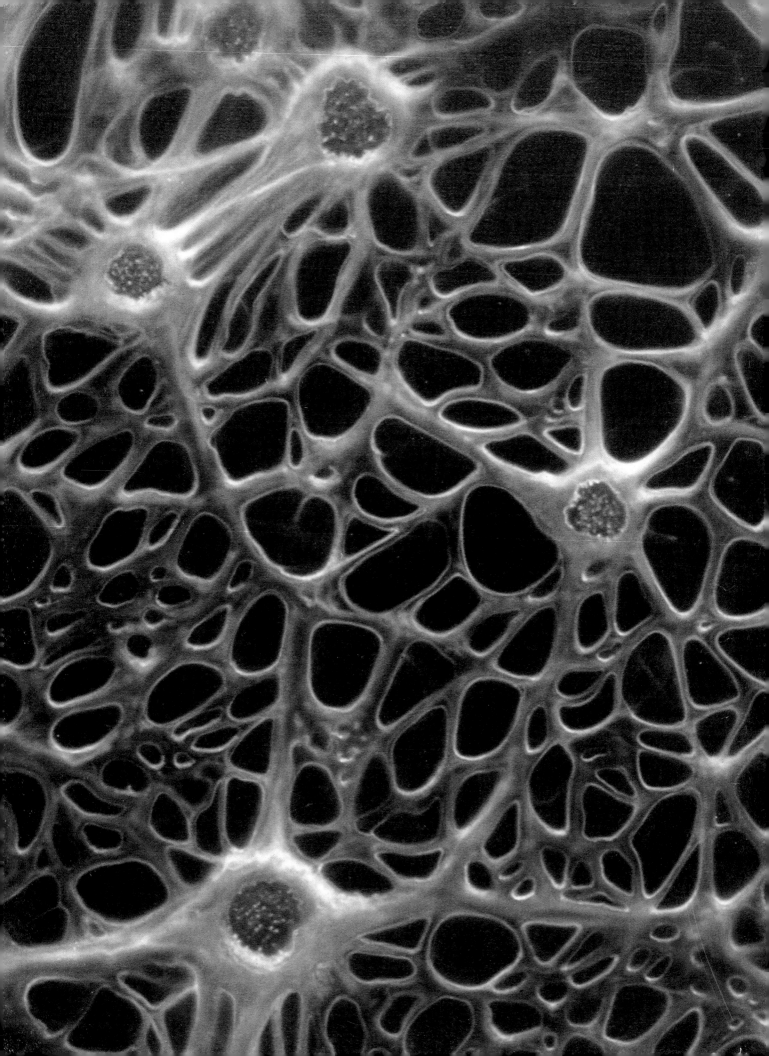

Introduction

Everything on Earth is either living or non-living. A lump of rock is non-living. If you plant it in the ground, it will not sprout and flower and make new little rocks in the same way that a living daffodil bulb will grow, flower and make new bulblets.

This is one essential characteristic of a living thing – it is able to reproduce itself to keep the species going. A living thing also needs food to grow and to keep its body working properly.

All living things, plants and animals alike, are made up of many tiny cells, in which the chemical processes of life take place. Collections of different cells form the tissues and organs that make up the bodies of plants and animals. Plants can manufacture their own food, but animals have to eat food to provide the energy for such activities as movement.

◄ Nerve cells growing in tissue culture in a laboratory. Nerve cells are the key to all nervous systems. They carry information from the muscles and skin to the brain and spinal cord.

The basis of life

Spot facts

- The human body produces an average of 9,000 million red blood cells every hour.

- In large animals, individual nerve cells can be up to 1 m in length.

- The largest single-celled organism is a kind of alga called the mermaid's wineglass. It can be up to 7 cm long.

- One cubic millimetre of brain tissue contains about 50,000 nerve cells.

- Every plant and animal uses the same chemical molecule to store information about itself. This molecule, called DNA, is found inside every single cell.

Every living thing is made up of basic units called cells. The smallest plants and animals consist of only a single cell. Larger organisms are made up of many cells. Animals and plants have developed specialist cells which perform particular tasks. Groups of similar types of cells make up the various tissues and organs of the body. However, all cells have a similar structure that enables them to carry out the basic functions of life.

▶ Flat cells from the skin that lines the human cheeks. They have been stained green, with the cell nuclei stained orange so that they can be studied under a microscope.

6

Cells in plants

The cells in both plants and animals have the same basic structure and organization. They consist of a blob of jelly-like substance inside a flexible skin. The jelly is called cytoplasm, and the skin is the cell membrane. The cytoplasm contains several different parts, or organelles. They include a single nucleus, many mitochondria and a network called the endoplasmic reticulum. The nucleus is the cell's information and control centre, and the mitochondria produce energy.

There are also several basic differences between plant and animal cells. Plant cells have an additional cell wall outside the membrane. It is made of a tough substance called cellulose. The rigid walls protect and support the cells and give them their shape. Inside a plant cell there is usually a large space, called a vacuole. It is filled with a sugary liquid known as cell sap. Inside the cells in the green parts of plants there are chloroplasts. They contain the green pigment chlorophyll. Chloroplasts enable plants to use the energy of sunlight to make food, and to store it as starch.

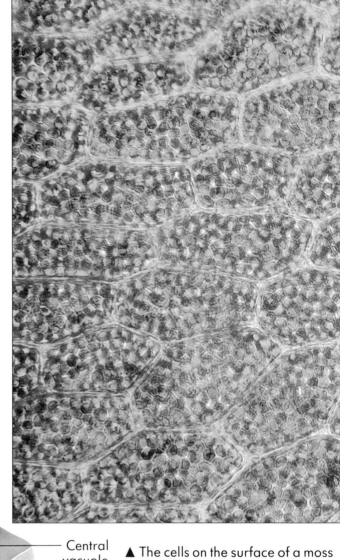

Plant cell

Central vacuole

Mitochondrion

Chloroplast

Cytoplasm

Nucleus

Endoplasmic reticulum

Cell membrane

▲ The cells on the surface of a moss leaf show up under a microscope. The green areas are chloroplasts.

◄ The nucleus controls the other parts of the cell. The chloroplasts and mitochondria work very closely together to produce the food and energy the cell requires. The endoplasmic reticulum makes complex molecules, such as proteins. It does so by assembling molecules of simple chemicals (amino acids) in the correct order. The large vacuole is usually kept full of cell sap, which provides the cell with an internal pressure. This pressure keeps the cell "inflated", in the same way that air pressure keeps a balloon inflated.

Cells in animals

Among the largest and most complex animal cells are those of the protozoa, or single-celled animals. All protozoa are highly organized, and their single cell can perform all the tasks necessary for independent life. A vacuole is used to digest food. Some protozoa have "hairs" or "tails", which they flick back and forth to produce movement.

The simplest multi-celled animals, such as jellyfish, consist of just two layers of cells. These two layers give the animal an inside, where food is digested, and an outside, which provides shape. But there is no room for any internal parts within the animal. All more complex animals have at least three layers of cells. It is the middle layers that normally develop specialized functions.

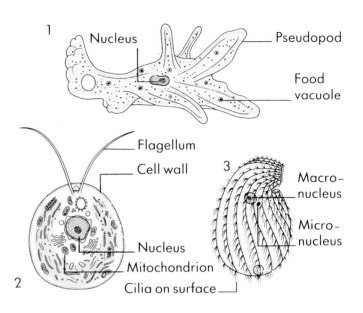

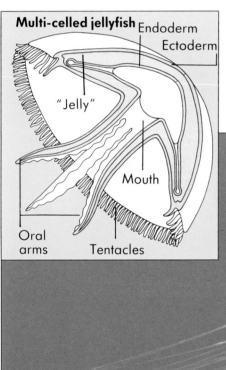

◀ The jellyfish has two layers of cells. The outer layer is called the ectoderm; and the inner layer, the endoderm. Between these is a jelly-like substance. Jellyfish have some specialist cells in the tentacles, which provide the animals with their sting.

▲ The amoeba (1) is one of the simplest forms of independent animal life, and has no definite shape. The more complex protozoa (2 and 3), have a definite shape, which is usually related to the normal direction of movement.

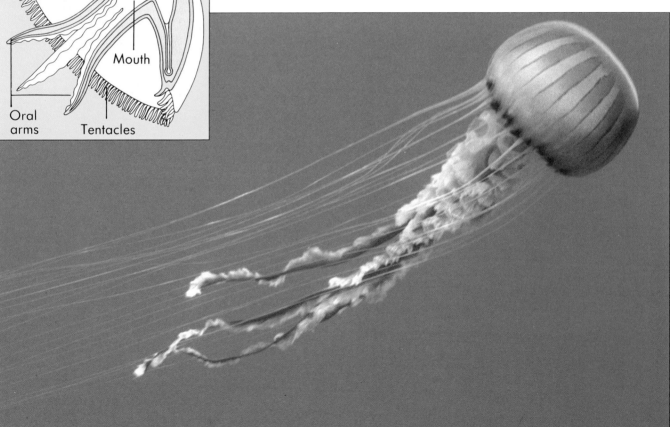

All animal cells are broadly the same and work in a similar way. They are made up of a jelly-like cytoplasm, kept inside a protective skin of membrane. The most important part, or organelle, within the cell is the nucleus. It is separated from the cytoplasm by a membrane. It gives instructions to the other parts of the cell. These carry out different functions, such as processing food into energy, or manufacturing the proteins that the cell needs for repairs and for living.

The cytoplasm is not a formless jelly, but contains a maze of folded membranes and threads of protein. These make up the cell's "skeleton". Some of the organelles, such as the mitochondria, have a distinct shape. They can be seen under the microscope as tiny dots.

Others are spread throughout the cytoplasm and do not have such a definite shape.

In all large animals, from earthworms to mammals, cells have grouped together to form tissues. For example, skin cells form skin; bone cells form bones. The different tissues, in turn, are further organized into organs and systems. For example, various nerve tissues work together in the nervous system; various bones connect together to form the skeleton.

The cells that make up the different tissues are different from one another, but all share the same basic structure. Each cell is a tiny, but very complicated, chemical factory. None of the cells, tissues or organs can exist independently of the others. Life is possible only when the separate components work together.

▼ Animal cells do not have chloroplasts or a rigid cell wall. The outer membrane comes into direct contact with adjacent cells. The vacuoles in animal cells are much smaller than in plant cells. Animal cytoplasm contains folded membranes and threads of protein.

Animal cell

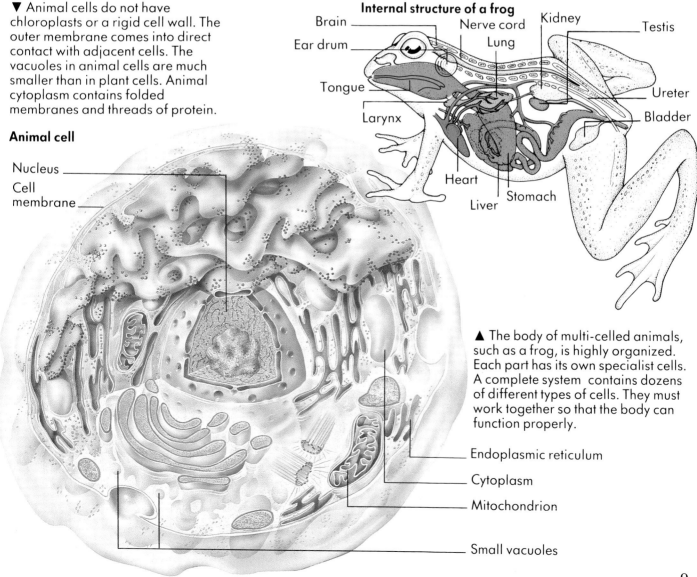

Nucleus
Cell membrane

Internal structure of a frog

Brain
Ear drum
Tongue
Larynx
Nerve cord
Lung
Kidney
Testis
Ureter
Bladder
Heart
Liver
Stomach

▲ The body of multi-celled animals, such as a frog, is highly organized. Each part has its own specialist cells. A complete system contains dozens of different types of cells. They must work together so that the body can function properly.

Endoplasmic reticulum

Cytoplasm

Mitochondrion

Small vacuoles

9

Specialist cells

Apart from the lowliest creatures, all animals have areas of specialized cell tissue to allow them to carry out specific tasks. Bones, blood, muscles and nerves, for example, all contain different kinds of cells. They look very different from each other when examined under a powerful microscope.

Bone consists largely of mineral substances such as phosphate salts of calcium, bound together with threads of protein. But it also contains millions of living cells. These cells have a very intricate outer surface. This allows them to form a living mesh through the non-living mineral structure.

Blood consists mostly of a watery solution called plasma, which contains many dissolved chemicals. Two kinds of cell form the living part of blood – red and white. The red cells give blood its colour and carry oxygen. They live for only four months before they are replaced. They are carried around the body by the blood system. The white cells can move independently of the flow of blood. There are many kinds of white cells and their function is to fight infection and to dispose of dead cells. The white cells can squeeze themselves out of the blood and move to all other parts of the body.

Muscle cells can change their shape by contracting (becoming smaller) and relaxing back to their original shape and size. There are three basic types of muscle cell. The cells in the heart are designed to move rhythmically without any instructions from outside. Smooth muscle cells, such as those in the stomach, often move of their own accord, but much more slowly. The cells that make up ordinary muscles are called striated cells. They take the form of long fibres with a striped appearance. These muscle cells can move only when they receive instructions from nerve cells.

Nerve cells called neurones carry messages in the body. In animals with backbones, the messages are mainly controlled by a large mass of star-shaped nerve cells called the brain.

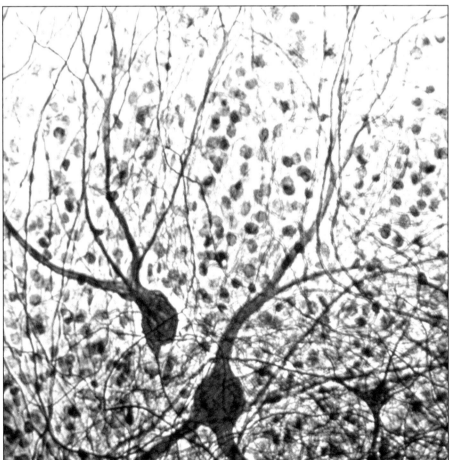

◄ The filaments (dendrites) of a nerve cell link an axon of one nerve cell to a dendrite of another. The connection is known as a synapse.

▼ The impulse that travels along a nerve's axon is electrical. A sheath of special cells keeps the axon insulated, so that none of the nerve impulse is lost.

Nerve cell

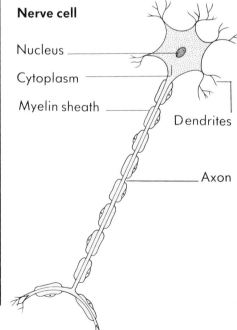

Nucleus

Cytoplasm

Myelin sheath

Dendrites

Axon

Neurones receive incoming messages from any one of a number of thin filaments known as dendrites. The message is passed on in one direction only by a long fibre called an axon. The axon is a long filament of cytoplasm that ends in a knob which sends a chemical message over the gap, called the synapse, to the next neurone.

The supplementary type of nerve cell does not carry messages. Some form a protective sheath around the axons of neurones, others perform more specialized functions within the brain.

All the other organs of the body (eyes, lungs, liver, and so on) also contain areas of specialized cell tissue to carry out their specific tasks.

The nucleus of a cell contains a complex molecule known as DNA (deoxyribonucleic acid). Cells duplicate by dividing into two. When this occurs, the nucleus breaks down and the DNA forms paired segments called chromosomes. Each chromosome is made up of a series of bands, or genes. With the exception of sex cells, all cells have paired sets of chromosomes.

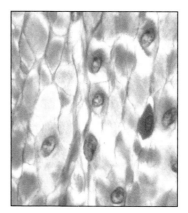 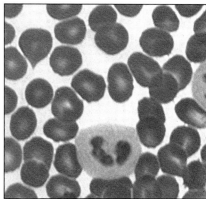

▲ A mass of smooth muscle tissue from the gut of a cat. Smooth muscle is designed to move quite slowly, and it is mostly found in the digestive system. The cells (left) are arranged in lines so that when they contract, they all pull in the same direction. The nucleus is clearly visible.

▲ Human blood cells. The small red blood cells (right) have a short lifespan, during which their main task is to transport oxygen molecules around the body. The larger blood cell is part of the body's defence mechanism.

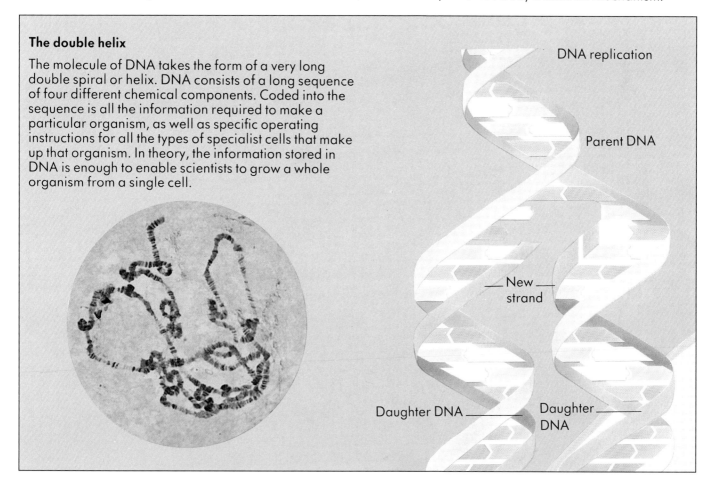

The double helix

The molecule of DNA takes the form of a very long double spiral or helix. DNA consists of a long sequence of four different chemical components. Coded into the sequence is all the information required to make a particular organism, as well as specific operating instructions for all the types of specialist cells that make up that organism. In theory, the information stored in DNA is enough to enable scientists to grow a whole organism from a single cell.

DNA replication

Parent DNA

New strand

Daughter DNA

Daughter DNA

Sex and reproduction

Spot facts

- For a fish egg, the odds against survival can be as high as a million to one. That is why some fish lay over 300 million at a time.

- An ostrich egg can weigh nearly 14 kg. It can support the weight of an adult human without breaking.

- In mammals, the time it takes for the young to develop in the womb before birth is remarkably varied. The deer mouse, for example, gives birth three to four weeks after mating, whereas a female elephant carries her calf for 22 months.

All living things – plants, animals and even bacteria – have only a limited lifespan. Unless a species can reproduce itself, it soon dies out. The simplest form of reproduction is asexual (without sex). It involves just one parent, and it produces exact duplicates of that parent. Sexual reproduction on the other hand involves two parents, a male and a female. A new organism is formed when a male sperm and a female egg join together.

▶ Snails mating. Each snail has both male and female sex organs. In theory, a snail could reproduce itself without a partner. In practice, a snail mates with another snail so that they can exchange DNA.

Reproduction without sex

Many single-celled organisms, such as an amoeba, reproduce in the same way that cells multiply. The process is known as binary fission. The cell divides into two halves, each with its own nucleus, which then separate and live as new individuals. Some simple multi-celled organisms, such as the hydra and some sponges, reproduce by budding. Buds grow on the outside of the parent body. They detach themselves when they are big enough for an independent existence.

Most plants reproduce sexually. This involves the male and female sex cells of two parents. There are, however, many plants that reproduce asexually, and some that alternate between both methods of reproduction. Plants such as fungi, mosses and ferns, scatter spores which go through an intermediate stage before developing into adult plants.

Other plants, such as strawberries, send out long shoots close to the ground which take root and grow into separate individuals. This method of asexual reproduction is called vegetative propagation. The additional bulbs and tubers produced by some plants, such as tulips and potatoes, are types of underground shoots which can also grow into new plants.

After asexual reproduction, the DNA of the new individual has come from a single parent. For this reason, the offspring and the parent share exactly the same genetic make-up and are therefore identical.

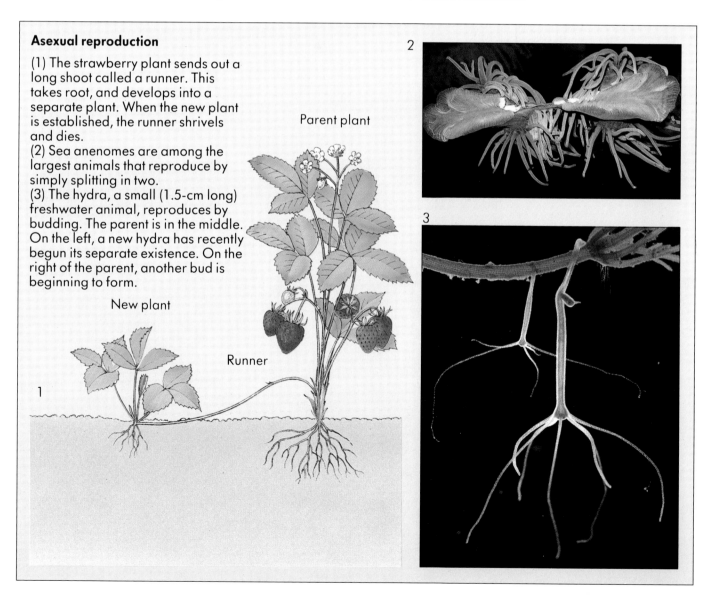

Asexual reproduction

(1) The strawberry plant sends out a long shoot called a runner. This takes root, and develops into a separate plant. When the new plant is established, the runner shrivels and dies.

(2) Sea anenomes are among the largest animals that reproduce by simply splitting in two.

(3) The hydra, a small (1.5-cm long) freshwater animal, reproduces by budding. The parent is in the middle. On the left, a new hydra has recently begun its separate existence. On the right of the parent, another bud is beginning to form.

Parent plant

New plant

Runner

1

2

3

Flowers

Most plants reproduce sexually, and flowers contain a plant's sex organs. The male organs are called stamens. At the end of each stamen, anthers produce the male sex cells. These are contained in grains of pollen. The female organ is formed of the stigma, style and ovary. At the centre of the ovary are one or more ovules each containing a female egg.

The transfer of pollen from the male stamens to the stigma is known as pollination. Depending on the species of plant, the pollen can come from the same flower, a different flower on the same plant, or from a completely separate plant.

When a pollen grain grows to reach the ovary, some of its contents join the egg cells to create a single cell. This process is known as fertilization. After fertilization the new single cell multiplies and develops into a seed containing a newly developing plant and a store of food.

Pollination and fertilization

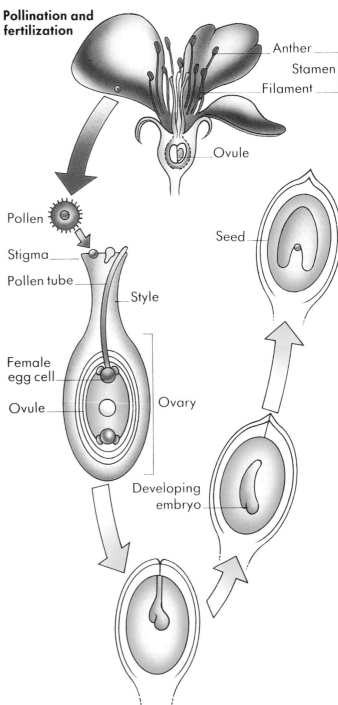

▲ Pollination and fertilization. Pollination occurs when an insect or the wind carries a pollen grain from the anther of one flower to the stigma of another. There it grows a pollen tube, which carries the male cell to the female egg cell in the ovule. They join together and fertilization occurs. The fertilized egg develops into an embryo, which with the ovule, grows into a seed.

◄ The lower flowers of the Rosebay willowherb open before the upper ones. This prevents self-pollination from flowers that are higher up the stem.

Laying eggs

All the more advanced species of animal reproduce sexually. The male sex cells are called sperm, and the female sex cells, eggs.

Fertilization occurs when a sperm joins with an egg to form a new single cell. Most animals lay their eggs, either before or after fertilization. Fish and amphibians use external fertilization. The female lays unfertilized eggs in water, and the male releases sperm to fertilize them. As soon as the embryo is sufficiently developed, the soft-skinned eggs hatch into young called larvae under water.

Fish larvae grow directly into adult fish. Amphibian larvae, however, go through a dramatic change called metamorphosis. The whole body alters completely as the animal changes from a water-breathing creature into an air-breathing one.

Reptiles and birds use internal fertilization. The eggs are fertilized inside the female body before they are laid. Tough, waterproof shells prevent the eggs from drying out. The embryo, or newly forming animal, develops into a miniature adult inside the egg before it hatches.

▼ A bird's egg provides a secure environment for the developing chick. The embryo gets nourishment from the egg yolk, which is entirely consumed by the time of hatching. A thick layer of albumen (egg-white) protects the embryo from vibration.

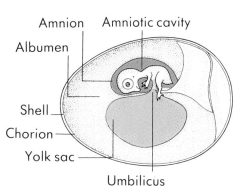

Amnion   Amniotic cavity

Albumen

Shell

Chorion

Yolk sac

Umbilicus

▲ A female Australian shield bug guards her eggs. All insects lay eggs. Some lay them on land and some in water. Eggs laid on land hatch into air-breathing larvae. For example, butterfly eggs hatch into air-breathing caterpillars. The larvae of insects that lay their eggs in water, such as water beetles, have to be able to breathe under water.

◀ Eggs of a Chinese alligator. The female Chinese alligator lays between 15 and 80 hard-shelled eggs. She remains with the eggs until they hatch 2 to 3 months later. When they first hatch, baby alligators are about 20 cm long. They grow about 30 cm a year until they reach maturity after 6 years.

Development of the embryo

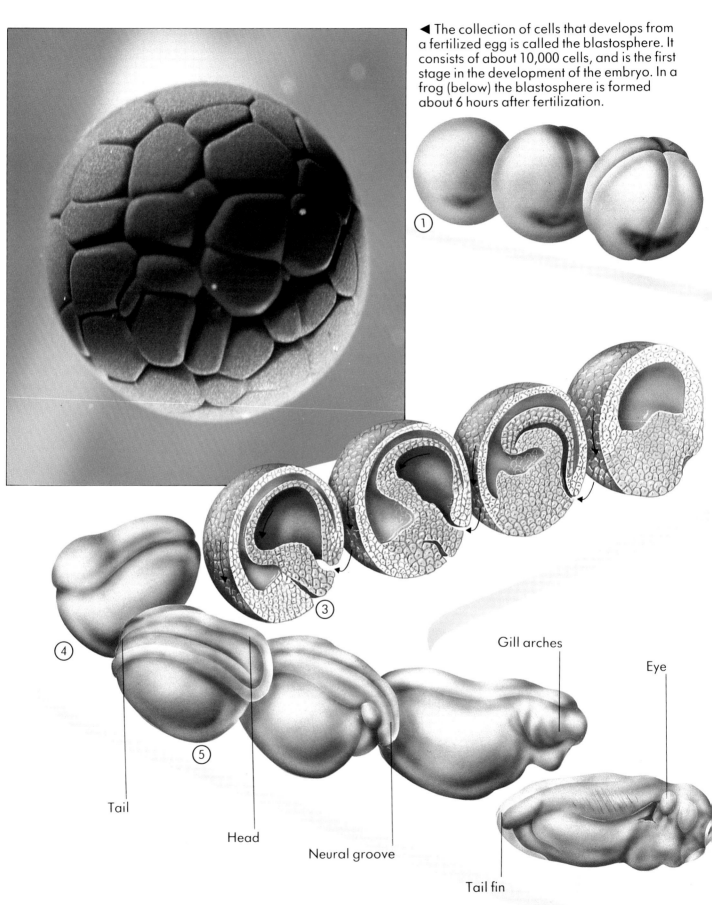

◀ The collection of cells that develops from a fertilized egg is called the blastosphere. It consists of about 10,000 cells, and is the first stage in the development of the embryo. In a frog (below) the blastosphere is formed about 6 hours after fertilization.

①

③

④

⑤

Gill arches

Eye

Tail

Head

Neural groove

Tail fin

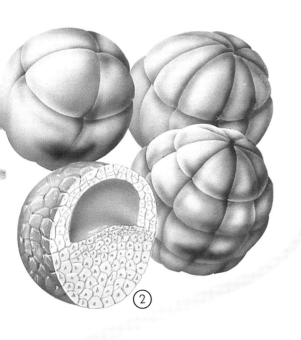

In most animals, the stages of development immediately after fertilization are exactly the same. The newly fertilized egg cell is known as a zygote. It duplicates itself by dividing in two, until it has developed into a hollow sphere of cells known as a blastosphere. The cells then stop multiplying in a symmetrical pattern. From this point on, the cluster of cells is called an embryo.

Over a period of time, which varies from animal to animal, the embryo gradually begins to take on a definite shape. Clusters of specialist cells appear, which will eventually form the different organs of the body. The most important stage of development is the formation of the neural groove. The groove provides the basis for the nervous system. In vertebrates it develops into the backbone, spinal cord and brain. After the neural groove has formed, the head of the embryo starts to form, and many of the main organs begin to appear.

Newly hatched amphibian and fish larvae differ very little from the embryo stage. In birds and reptiles, the embryo continues to develop inside the egg until it is fully formed. Mammals do not lay eggs; instead, the embryo grows inside the female until it is fully developed.

A frog zygote (1) divides about every 30 minutes. After about 6 hours, a hollow blastosphere (2) has formed, and the cells stop dividing symmetrically. An opening appears in the outer wall of the blastosphere which then extends inwards, squashing the hollow interior almost flat. Four hours later, the embryo contains about 30,000 cells that are divided into three distinct layers (3). A full day after fertilization (4), the embryo has lost its spherical appearance and acquired an oval shape with two ends. During the next few days the head develops at one end of the neural groove (5), and the eyes, gills and tail start to form. About 10 days after fertilization, the fully formed embryo (6) is ready to hatch.

▼ A Green tree frog and spawn. Unlike other species of frogs that lay their eggs either on or below the surface of water, the female Green tree frog lays her batch of eggs in a nest of leaves above the water. When the eggs develop into larvae, they drop into the water below.

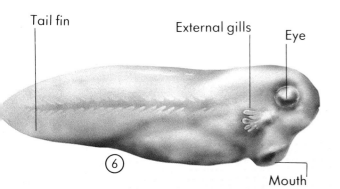

Tail fin   External gills   Eye

⑥

Mouth

Mammals

In mammals, fertilization occurs in or near the ovary, where the eggs are produced. The fertilized egg moves into the uterus (womb), where it becomes embedded in the soft lining tissue and develops into an embryo. As the embryo grows, a special organ called the placenta develops alongside it. The placenta is joined to the embryo by an umbilical cord. This connects the embryo to the mother's blood supply, and enables it to receive the nourishment it needs to keep growing. After a period of time (in humans, about 11 weeks), the cells in the embryo have developed into all the organs of the adult animal. The embryo is now described as a foetus.

` The foetus continues to grow inside the mother for the full period of gestation, or pregnancy. When fully developed, the new mammal passes out of the mother's body, and is born. Some newborn mammals, such as antelopes, are able to stand up immediately after birth and run with their mothers. In other mammals, including humans, the newborn young are completely helpless and require a great deal of care from the mother. Young mammals cannot eat normal food, and feed on the milk produced by special glands inside the mother's body. This is known as suckling the young.

Sexual organs of a rabbit

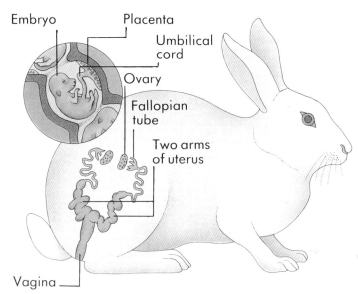

Embryo
Placenta
Umbilical cord
Ovary
Fallopian tube
Two arms of uterus
Vagina

▲ There is no room in the ovary for a growing foetus. The fertilized egg travels down a tube to the uterus, where the cells that will develop into the placenta are located. The mother and foetus do not share the same blood. The placenta allows substances to pass from the blood of the mother to that of the foetus.

► Sperms clustering around an egg. The first sperm to enter the egg sets off a reaction that prevents the others from entering the egg. Identical twins occur when an embryo splits into two and each group of cells forms a genetically identical baby.

Duck-billed platypus

The duck-billed platypus of Australia is one of only three species of mammals that lay eggs. It is probably a direct descendant of primitive mammals that evolved before those with a placenta first appeared. When the young hatch, they are very underdeveloped and can hardly move. The platypus has other primitive features which mammals have since improved upon. The glands that produce milk have no nipples for the young to suck. The milk just oozes from tiny openings on the mother's belly. The other egg-laying mammals are spiny anteaters (echidnas), which are also found only in Australia and on nearby islands.

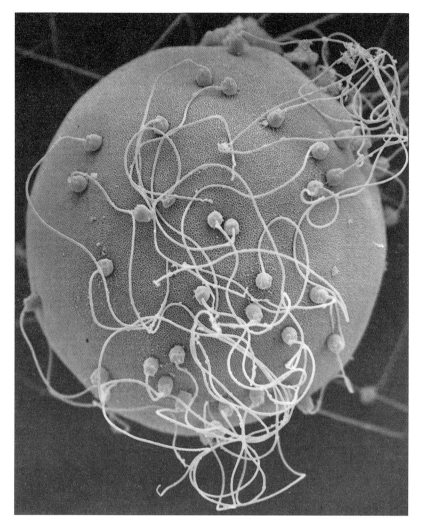

▲ Piglets feeding. Young mammals cannot feed on solid food, and so they are dependent on their mother for the milk she produces. The mother's milk provides all the necessary nourishment for the piglets to survive and grow.

◀ A deer giving birth. Young deer are born out in the open, and can stand up within a few hours of being born. But they still require a lot of attention immediately after birth. Constant licking soon clears the nostrils so that breathing is not impaired. The cleaning process also stimulates the eyes and ears. In the wild, young animals must quickly learn to be alert for the slightest sign of danger. By comparison, young cats are helpless, and do not open their eyes for several days.

Energy for living

Spot facts

- *An elephant devours its own weight in food every month. A snake may only eat its own weight during a whole year. Some seabirds consume their own weight in fish every day.*

- *Some birds and reptiles swallow pebbles, which are used to grind up tough food they have eaten.*

- *Ants keep other insects called aphids like humans keep cattle. They "milk" them for a sweet liquid known as honeydew.*

- *The Australian mountain ash, a type of eucalyptus tree, grows as much as 14 m in only two years.*

▶ A flycatcher feeding its young. Food is needed for growth, and young animals have huge appetites. Those that cannot feed themselves, such as young birds and mammals, must be fed by the parents. Many young animals cannot eat the same type of food as the adults. Birds often feed their young on food they have partly digested.

Life requires a constant supply of energy. Even during rest or sleep, energy is required to power the internal systems of an organism. Energy is obtained by processing food. Plants manufacture their own food from simple chemicals they take in from their surroundings. But animals need to eat food. Some eat plants, others eat other animals. Whatever the source of the food, it is converted into energy, usually by combining it with oxygen inside each cell. Nearly all organisms have a system for taking oxygen into their bodies. Eating can be an occasional activity, but breathing must be a continual process if the organism is to stay alive.

Food for plants

Plants are the vital link in the cycle of food and energy that connects all life on Earth. A plant does not need to feed directly, but makes its own food from simple chemicals by a process called photosynthesis. Plants do not have any special organs for feeding. Each green plant cell contains all that is needed to produce and store food. These cells, known as chloroplasts, are usually concentrated in the leaves.

The type of food that is made by photosynthesis is sugar. It is one kind of carbohydrate. Much of the food is stored, either as sugary cell sap, or as starch, a more concentrated form of carbohydrate. The rest is consumed. The mitochondria in the cells convert some carbohydrate into energy, which is used to fuel further chemical reactions. These break down the rest of the carbohydrates and combine them with water and minerals to produce other substances the plant requires.

To convert carbohydrates back into energy, the mitochondria require oxygen. The conversion process produces carbon dioxide as a waste product. During daytime photosynthesis, there is an exchange of waste gases between the mitochondria and the chloroplasts. But far more oxygen is produced than is required, and this is released back into the atmosphere.

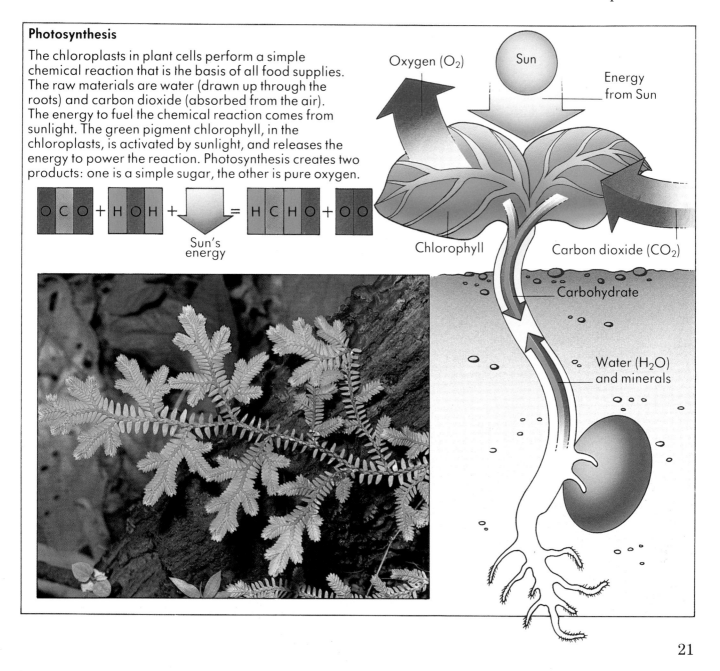

Photosynthesis

The chloroplasts in plant cells perform a simple chemical reaction that is the basis of all food supplies. The raw materials are water (drawn up through the roots) and carbon dioxide (absorbed from the air). The energy to fuel the chemical reaction comes from sunlight. The green pigment chlorophyll, in the chloroplasts, is activated by sunlight, and releases the energy to power the reaction. Photosynthesis creates two products: one is a simple sugar, the other is pure oxygen.

Oxygen (O₂)

Sun

Energy from Sun

Sun's energy

Chlorophyll

Carbon dioxide (CO₂)

Carbohydrate

Water (H₂O) and minerals

Food for animals

Animals are much more complex organisms than plants. They require far more energy to survive than could be directly provided by the Sun. They get their energy by consuming food. All multi-celled animals have specialized structures or systems for processing food. The absorption of food is called digestion. Digestion involves both mechanical and chemical processes. In most animals, these processes are carried out by the digestive system.

Food for animals is made up of various substances which are essential in order to live. But not all animals eat them in the same proportions, and some have very specialized eating habits. The mitochondria in animal cells use carbohydrates to produce energy in the same way as those in plant cells. In addition, animals can make use of fats, which are a much more efficient way of storing energy. Fats can be converted back into energy. They can also be used to provide the body with an insulating layer to keep it warm in cold weather.

Animals use large amounts of various proteins in their structures. Many proteins can be manufactured by the body's chemical "factories", but an intake of some raw materials is necessary. The body also requires small amounts of vitamins and minerals.

Simple animals have a digestive system with a single opening. They take in food through the mouth, and it is dissolved by chemicals known as digestive juices so that it can be absorbed into the body. But most animals have a digestive system with two openings. Food taken in at one end is processed as it passes through the system. Waste matter is ejected at the other.

Some animals eat only plants and are known as herbivores. Cellulose, the tough material in plant cell walls, is very hard to digest. Herbivores have a complicated digestive system to break down the cellulose. Another group of animals, the carnivores, eat only meat. Meat is a more concentrated form of energy, so carnivores need to eat less often than herbivores.

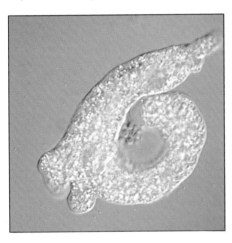

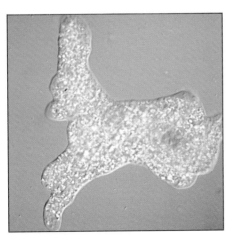

◄ An amoeba feeds by surrounding its food, and absorbing it directly into its body. Inside the cell, the food is contained within a vacuole, where it is broken down and absorbed. Anything that is not absorbed is left behind as the amoeba moves off. White blood cells consume bacteria and dead cells in the same way.

▼ The chameleon's tongue is just one of the extraordinary animal adaptations related to the essential task of getting enough food. The tongue is tipped with an area of cells that produce a sticky liquid. When the tongue is "fired" at an insect, a "hit" ensures that the insect is captured and energy is not wasted.

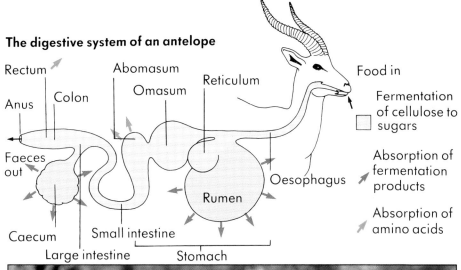

The digestive system of an antelope

Rectum

Anus

Colon

Abomasum

Omasum

Reticulum

Food in

Fermentation
of cellulose to
sugars

Faeces
out

Absorption of
fermentation
products

Oesophagus

Absorption of
amino acids

Rumen

Caecum

Small intestine

Large intestine

Stomach

◀ Considerable energy is required to break down cellulose. Many herbivores use bacteria to break down the cellulose in a process called fermentation. The bacteria have to be kept in a separate part of the stomach, otherwise the digestive juices would destroy them. Some animals, such as deer and cattle, chew their food twice, both before and after fermentation. Such animals are known as ruminants. After the second chewing, the food passes to the rest of the digestive system for further processing.

◀ Sable antelopes feeding. Grass has relatively little food value for its weight. Ruminants have to spend most of their waking hours feeding. They chew a mouthful of grass (known as the cud) until it is in a more digestible state.

▼ A bat feeding on nectar. Many plants produce nectar to attract the insects that are needed for pollination. Some birds and bats have also learned to exploit this food. Indeed, some tropical species feed only on nectar. The animals have adapted to their food supply by developing long tongues that can reach deep into the flowers. Their heads become covered with pollen, which is then spread to other flowers.

Meat-eaters

Some animals specialize in eating those parts of a plant that contain food in a more concentrated form such as the seeds and fruit. Other animals prefer an even more concentrated diet, and eat animal meat. Meat-eaters are known as carnivores, although sometimes a separate category (insectivores) is used for those that eat only insects. Carnivores eat both herbivores and other carnivores.

Animals represent a doubly valuable source of food. The hard work of converting plant cells into animal cells has already been done. In addition, animals contain much higher levels of proteins and fats than plants do.

The digestion of meat is a much quicker process than the digestion of vegetable food. For this reason, the digestive system of a carnivore is much shorter and simpler than that of a herbivore. In other respects, the digestive process is essentially the same in both types of animal. The processes of biting and chewing start to break down the food. The breakdown is continued by the muscle contractions that move the food along the gut. The many chemical processes of digestion take place in the stomach and small intestine. At every stage, the food is dissolved by acidic digestive juices and enzymes, chemicals that speed up the action of the digestive juices. The food can then be absorbed into the body.

▶ A python eating a rat. A snake must swallow its prey whole because it cannot chew its food. It can take weeks for a medium-sized animal to be digested. During this time the snake does not eat.

▼ The sundew traps insects with its sticky leaves. It grows in poor conditions and cannot get enough minerals from the soil. It gets them instead by breaking down insects and absorbing their juices.

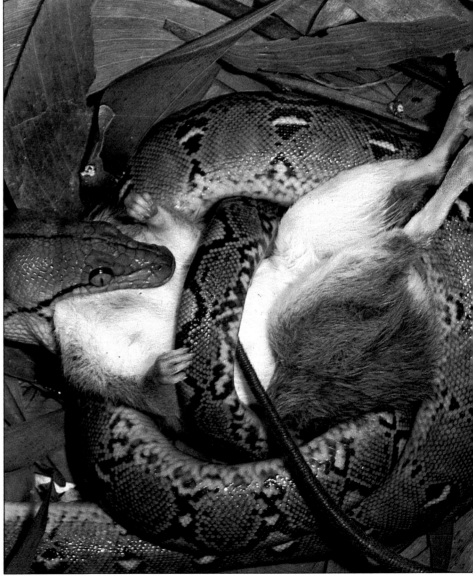

24

The first stage of digestion occurs in the mouth during chewing. Here the food is mixed with enzymes contained in saliva. In the stomach, the process is continued by various enzymes and acids. They break down the carbohydrates, proteins and fats into simpler forms. Only a tiny fraction of food is absorbed by the stomach. Most absorption occurs in the small intestine, where a further set of enzymes continue to act on the food. Eventually, all the carbohydrates are turned into simple sugars, and the proteins are broken down into amino acids. The large intestine, the part of the digestive system after the small intestine, absorbs water and some dissolved minerals.

▼ A large carnivore, such as a lion, needs to consume its own body weight of food every 10 days. When not feeding or hunting, lions spend most of their time resting to conserve energy. The cubs have to learn to tear their own food from the carcass, or they will starve. After about a year, the cubs are ready to hunt small animals for themselves.

Spiders and some insects use a method of external digestion. They inject their prey with saliva before eating it. The body of the prey is dissolved by the enzymes in the saliva, and the liquid food is sucked up through tubes.

Food chains
Plants are the only food producers on Earth. All animals eat plants either directly or indirectly. The food resources of the Earth are arranged in a series of food chains, all of which start with plants. For example, a caterpillar that eats leaves is in turn eaten by a small bird; the bird then lays eggs, which are eaten by a rat; the rat is in turn eaten by a hawk. There are countless different food chains. Together they make up what is known as the food web, which links together all forms of life.

When plants make food, they release oxygen into the atmosphere. As animals need oxygen to use food, this further reinforces the life-bond between plants and animals.

▲ Ticks and fleas have evolved a lifestyle outside the food web. They are parasites, and get their food by sucking the blood of other animals without killing them. Common parasites cause irritation but do not directly harm their hosts. Much more dangerous are internal parasites, such as tapeworms, which live inside the intestines of animals. They feed by absorbing the host's food. They can grow up to several metres long and are difficult to get rid of.

Breathing

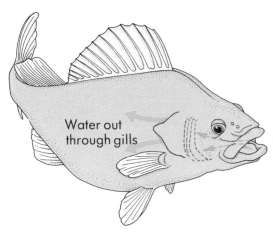

Water out through gills

Water in through mouth

▲ Flatworms, like jellyfish, do not have any special breathing apparatus. Their bodies are so thin, and their energy requirements so low, that the transfer of gases can take place directly through the animal's outer layer of cells.

▲ ▶ The gills of fishes and other underwater animals, such as crabs and shellfish, work in a similar way to lungs. Water is taken in through the mouth and passed through the gills, a series of feathery tissues. The gills are richly supplied with blood and the transfer of gases takes place on their surface. The water is then passed out of the body through the slits of the gill covers.

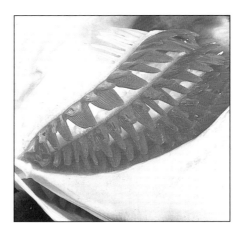

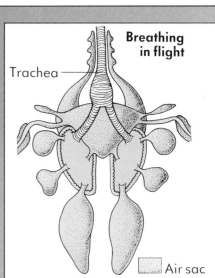

Breathing in flight

Trachea

☐ Air sac

▶ Whooper swans in flight. Flying requires tremendous amounts of energy. Birds have a series of air sacs connected to their lungs so that they can take in extra oxygen (above).

The mitochondria in every living cell need oxygen to convert food into energy. The waste product of the energy-producing reaction is carbon dioxide. The exchange of gases, breathing in oxygen and breathing out carbon dioxide, is known as respiration. Complex animals have developed special structures or organs for respiration. Most animals use blood to carry the gases around the body.

Insects breathe by drawing in air through a series of holes called spiracles in the sides of their bodies. The holes are connected to a series of minute tubes, which carry the air directly to the muscles. Only a small amount of oxygen is diverted to the bloodstream. Fishes use special organs called gills, which can extract dissolved oxygen from water.

All other air-breathing animals use lungs for the exchange of gases. The lungs are basically a series of cavities, surrounded by a network of blood vessels. Oxygen in the air is absorbed by the moist lining of the lungs, and passes into the bloodstream. The red cells in the blood carry the oxygen to all the other parts of the body. Carbon dioxide given off by the mitochondria is dissolved in the blood and carried back to the lungs. Then the process of absorption works in reverse, and the carbon dioxide passes into the lungs and is breathed out. Even plants have to breathe when they are not producing oxygen by photosynthesis. At night, when sunlight is not available for photosynthesis, plants absorb oxygen from the atmosphere and give off carbon dioxide, just like animals.

The senses

- *Insects can see movements that take place in as little as one-thousandth of a second.*

- *Even when blindfolded, bats can fly through a maze of wires less than 1 mm thick.*

- *Some snakes and mosquitoes can detect and home in on heat.*

- *In the deep sea some fish produce their own light to see by.*

- *A male moth's antennae may have up to 10,000 sensor cells. Each can detect a single molecule of the chemical substance given out by a female moth to attract a male.*

▶ The fox has good eyesight, although it sees everything in black and white. But a blind fox is much less helpless than a blind human being. The fox relies heavily on its keen sense of smell when hunting. Smells are not obscured by darkness or dense undergrowth. They can lead the animal directly to its prey.

Animals need information about their environment. They need to know when danger threatens, where food is available, and how to find a mate. They pick up this information through their senses. It is gathered by various specialized cells and is relayed to the brain. Without this vital information, animals would soon die out. In many animals, the senses form the basis for communication. Man has only five senses, sight, hearing, touch, smell and taste. Some animals have more.

28

Sight

Most organisms are sensitive to light. Plants turn the light into energy. Animals use clusters of light-sensitive cells to form a picture of the outside world. In many of the simpler animals, the picture is restricted to showing the difference between light and shade. But most animals have developed sophisticated light-gathering organs called eyes.

Eyes usually take the form of a ball of clear fluid. One side of the ball is transparent so that light can pass through the liquid to the far side. Dark-coloured receptor cells at the back of the eyeball turn the light into nerve impulses, which are passed to the brain. Most eyes are useful all-purpose organs. But many animals have a very highly developed sense of sight, which is adapted to their lifestyle.

▶ The large eyes of the Philippine tarsier allow it to see clearly even by the faintest starlight. Most animals that are nocturnal (active mainly at night) have very large eyes. The bigger the eyeball, the more light it lets in.

▼ The Common buzzard hunts from above. Most of its prey consists of small mammals such as rabbits. When the buzzard looks down, it is looking through the equivalent of a telescope. Its eyes magnify things about eight times, so that even the smallest prey is visible.

Ways of seeing

Animals need only one pair of eyes to give them a sense of sight. Those that have more, such as spiders and some insects, generally use only one pair to detect shape and movement. The other pairs of "eyes" are simple clusters of cells that do not assist vision, but merely respond to changes in the strength of light.

Insects are unique in having developed compound eyes, which have all the receptor cells on the outside surface. The eye of a dragonfly, for example, has more than 30,000 separate cells. Each cell is connected to the brain by its own nerve. Compound eyes provide insects with remarkable all-round vision. An insect does not have to turn its head to follow a moving object. In this way compound eyes help the insect track prey and avoid predators.

All vertebrates have complex eyes, which contain a lens to focus the light, and an opening called an iris to control the amount of light entering the eye. These components enable the eye to operate effectively at all levels of natural light. The light is focused on to a layer of light-sensitive cells at the back of the eyeball called the retina. The retina assembles the light into a detailed picture, which is sent to the brain down the optic nerve. The brain adjusts the picture by sending nerve impulses back to the muscles in the eye.

Not all the receptor cells are the same. Some are especially sensitive at low levels of light. In nocturnal animals, most of the retina is composed of low-light receptors. These animals tend to have extremely poor colour vision.

Kinds of eyes

The compound eye (right) is adapted to life at the insect level. It can detect small, fast movements at ranges up to 30 m. Reptiles (below) and mammals (bottom) can adjust the size of the iris to compensate for the amount of available light.

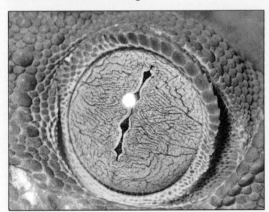

Seeing underwater

Life in the seas presents special problems with seeing. Light is absorbed by water. Very little light penetrates below depths of 150 m. Blue light penetrates the farthest. As a result, many deep-sea fish have adopted a red coloration so that they are almost invisible in the blue light. To overcome this, some deep-sea predators have evolved eyes that are especially sensitive. Some of them have up to five layers of receptor cells. Others have developed the ability to generate red light to illuminate their prey.

The octopus has by far the most highly developed eyes of any invertebrate. Octopus eyes are just as complex as those of a mammal, if not more so. Each eye can focus and move independently and look in a completely different direction.

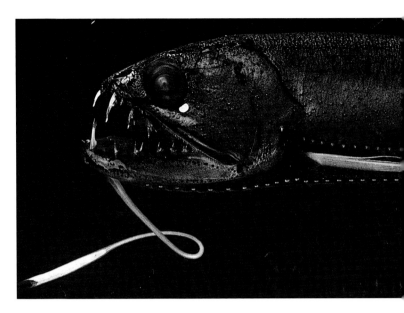

▼ Mexican cave fish have adapted to a life of darkness and have lost their eyes completely. Life could not have evolved very far without eyes, but over many generations they can be lost through lack of use. Most of the 38 other species of cave fish are blind.

▲ Some deep-sea predators dangle clusters of luminous bacteria as bait to attract their prey. Others, like this one, are more active in their pursuit of food. The bacteria are incorporated in special organs in the head and are used like underwater searchlights.

Hearing and touch

Sound waves can do many things that light waves cannot. They can travel equally well by day or night. They can travel round corners. They are not as easily obscured by vegetation. But sound waves of movement carry very little useful information. In general, the sense of hearing has evolved alongside the ability to generate and make use of sounds. Among vertebrates, only birds and mammals have a well-developed sense of hearing. Most birds and mammals use sound to communicate with each other. This communication is often limited to simple signals of alarm and distress.

Sound waves are gathered by the ears. They are then amplified by a series of tiny bones and very fine membranes. The receptor cells are deep in the ear. They have hairs that are sensitive to the slightest movement in the fluid around them. These movements are transmitted to the brain, which identifies any significant patterns. Next to man, birds make the most extensive use of the sense of hearing.

▼ Bats use a method of echo-location to hunt insects on the wing. They emit a series of very high frequency sounds, and listen carefully for any echoes from nearby objects. Using this technique, bats can identify an insect at a distance of more than 50 cm in the dark.

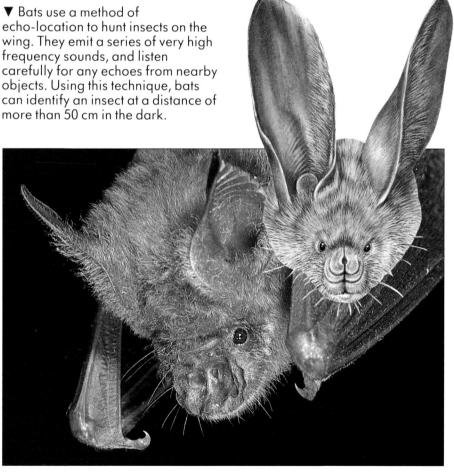

In vertebrates, the sense of touch is spread over the whole of the skin surface. Receptor cells, which are sensitive to movement or pressure, send impulses from all parts of the body. Many animals have special adaptations to amplify the sense of touch. Mammals often have sensitive whiskers projecting from around the mouth and nose. Some fish have short tentacles, which are used to feel for food in murky water. Birds usually have very little use for a well-developed sense of touch.

Among the advanced invertebrates, the sense of touch is usually much more restricted because the hard covering of these animals is not usually equipped with receptor cells. A spider however, has extremely sensitive hairs on its legs, which it positions on its web. When an insect lands in the web, the vibrations are sent along the thread and alert the spider.

Insects rely on their antennae for a sense of touch. Insect antennae also smell and taste the environment. The senses of smell and taste are very closely linked, and depend upon the ability of receptor cells to detect certain molecules. In most cases, receptors in the mouth sample food; those in the nose sample the air.

Many mammals that hunt their food rely strongly on their sense of smell. As well as detecting the scent of prey on the wind, they can follow a scent trail along the ground. The sense of smell can be used to give information about the past. By sniffing over a piece of ground, a fox or a badger can tell which other animals have passed by recently.

◀ A Fennec fox. In the desert, sound is of particular importance because life is so sparse, and every movement is significant. The large, well-developed ears of the desert fox enable the animal to determine the direction of a distant sound with great accuracy.

▼ This mouse is straining all five of its senses to the utmost while engaged in the perilous task of collecting food. Animals that are prey to many predators are constantly alert for the slightest sign of danger, and move only with extreme caution.

Special senses

Human beings have only five senses. But many animals inhabit a world of sensation that man can only visit by using scientific instruments. Insects are extremely good at detecting and producing minute traces of certain chemicals. Social insects, such as ants and termites, use such chemicals as a means of communicating simple messages. Other insects, notably moths, use chemicals known as pheromones to attract mates from great distances.

Some fish can generate a weak electrical field around themselves. An approaching fish causes minute changes in the field which can be detected. But this underwater sense is primitive compared to that of some sea-living mammals. Whales and dolphins have complex organs in their heads to send and receive sounds underwater. These sounds are used for echo-location while hunting, and are effective over great distances. They are also used for mapping the ocean bottom as an aid to navigation. Whales and dolphins also use sounds for communication. The Humpback whale is noted for the complex "songs" it sings, which can carry for up to 30 km. Dolphins are thought to have a whole language of high-pitched chirps.

Homing pigeons have the uncanny ability to navigate accurately over long distances. For many years, exactly how they did this was a mystery, but it has been discovered that the birds have a built-in compass. Tiny clusters of cells in the bird's skull and neck muscles were found to contain specks of magnetic minerals. These are thought to act as a compass needle, giving the pigeon a constant pointer to the north. Other birds appear to navigate by fixed points, such as landmarks or stars.

Internal "clocks"

Many animals possess a built-in biological "clock". Some of these clocks are linked to periods of a day, others to a month or a year. The clocks are "set" by the movement of the Sun and the Moon. But they remain fairly accurate even if the animal is kept in darkness. Animals use these clocks to regulate their feeding and breeding behaviour.

Other special senses are extensions of ordinary abilities. Some animals can detect light that is outside the visible spectrum. Bees are sensitive to ultraviolet light. They can see patterns on flowers invisible to human eyes. The patterns usually point towards the nectar, encouraging the bee to pollinate the flower.

▼ Some snakes, such as the rattlesnake and pit viper, have clusters of heat-sensitive cells above the mouth. These cells enable the snakes to detect warm-blooded prey, even in total darkness.

▶ The crayfish can sense the direction of gravity. Special organs at the base of the antennae contain grains of sand surrounded by sensitive hairs. These organs tell the animal which way it is swimming.

Homing in

Many birds regularly migrate over thousands of kilometres. It is believed that they navigate by using the Sun and the stars. At night in the Northern Hemisphere, the Pole star indicates true north. By day, birds such as homing pigeons allow for the movement of the Sun, and alter course accordingly.

▲ A male moth can sense the pheromones of a female more than 10 km away, if the wind is in the right direction. The feathery antennae contain thousands of special receptors, each capable of detecting a single molecule of pheromone.

▼ A dace. Fish have clusters of sensitive cells called the lateral line arranged down the mid-line of the body. These cells can detect changes in current flow and water pressure.

On the move

• When threatened, a midge can increase the speed of its wing-beats to more than 130,000 beats a minute.

• A cheetah can accelerate from a standing start to 72 km/h in just 2 seconds.

• Fleas can jump up to 350 times their own length. This is equivalent to a person making a single jump of over 600 m.

• Elephants can charge at speeds of up to 40 km/h.

▶ The sidewinder snake is well named, because it moves sideways. Snakes move by flexing their bodies from side to side. Their ribs are attached to hardened scales on the underside of the body. While the scales at the rear of the body dig into the ground, the rest of the body can be pushed forwards. The front scales then dig in, and the rear portion is pulled along.

For both plants and animals, the ability to move can make the difference between life and death. Plants can make slight movements in response to their environment. They adjust the position of their leaves, for example, to get the full benefit of the Sun. But movement as a form of transport is confined to animals, which have developed different methods of using muscles to move about freely.

Simple movements

Plant movement is largely confined to growth, but plants can control the direction of growth to a large extent. From the moment that they sprout from seeds, plants are sensitive to gravity. They send their shoots up towards the surface of the soil, and their roots downwards in search of water.

Once a plant has emerged into the open air, its growth is directed towards the sunlight. This ensures that it receives the greatest possible energy for photosynthesis. Special cells produce chemicals called auxins, which pass down the stem and affect the growth rate of particular groups of cells. For instance, the faster growth of cells on one side of a stem makes the stem curve away from that side.

Plants can also make other small movements, such as tilting their leaves to follow the Sun, opening and closing flowers and curling up leaves if they are touched. They do this by emptying sap from some of their cells. Without the sap to keep them inflated, the plant bends. This is why plants droop when short of water.

Single-celled movement

An amoeba moves by flowing into itself in the direction of travel. Other microscopic organisms have developed special structures for movement through water. Some have long flagella, like tiny whips, which push the organism along. Other have developed hair-like cilia, which are used to give a rowing effect.

◄ The tiny *Paramecium* has one of the most complicated systems of movement of any single-celled organism. The cilia round its rim are moved in unison to row the animal through the water. Cilia are also used by many larger animals to move liquids through internal organs.

▼ Fungi provide some of the most dramatic examples of plant movement. This stinkhorn fungus grows to its full height of nearly 20 cm in only four hours. The pictures below were taken at hourly intervals. Most other plant movement, however, is much slower.

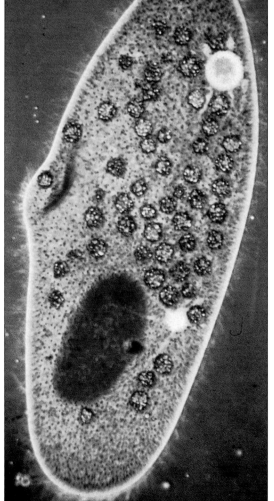

Movement on land

Animal movement comes from coordinated muscle power. Just as each muscle cell can change its shape, so whole muscle tissues can contract and relax. The muscles used in movement are attached to the skeleton, which is used like a series of levers.

Animals with an exoskeleton, or external skeleton, such as insects and crabs, have their muscles inside their skeletons. In vertebrates, the muscles are positioned around an internal skeleton. Most animals have special limbs with which they walk. These are tipped with hooks, claws, pincers, suckers or hands and feet to achieve a better grip.

Vertebrates have only four limbs, and most of them use all four when walking or running. Most birds move by flapping their wings and can move only slowly on their legs. But the flightless ostrich has developed extremely powerful legs. It can run at speeds of up to 80 km/h for about 30 minutes at a time. In contrast, the penguin normally waddles around at about 3 km/h. In an emergency, penguins sometimes lie down on their bellies and use all four limbs to help them toboggan across ice and snow at great speeds. Mammals have the most highly developed limbs. For their size they are the fastest and most agile of all animals.

▲ The cheetah is probably the fastest animal on Earth. It can reach speeds of up to 120 km/h over distances of a few hundred metres. The cheetah's speed is a result of very fast muscle movements, combined with an extremely long stride. A very flexible spine enables the cheetah to expand and contract its whole body.

◀ The orang-utan lives in trees where there is a constant danger of falling to the ground. It has therefore developed very strong flexible fingers and toes. Both hands and feet can be used to hold on to a branch, making it easier and safer to feed in the trees. Although the orang-utan is one of man's closest relatives, it walks on the ground using all four limbs.

None of the mammals can match the agility of some small lizards, such as the gecko. Adhesive pads on the bottom of each foot enable the gecko to climb up any sort of surface. It can even run across ceilings.

Many insects are very poor fliers, and scuttle around on their six legs. Some, such as grasshoppers and crickets, have developed very powerful hindlegs, and move in a series of leaps and bounds. They can jump up to 20 times their own body length. Spiders have eight legs and crabs have ten, but both use four pairs for walking. Some of the land crabs are also very good at climbing trees in search of food.

Muscle movement

Some invertebrates can move without any legs at all. Earthworms literally eat their way through the ground, taking in soil at one end and passing it out the other. The earthworm propels itself by using a group of muscular segments to brace itself against the tunnel wall. The rest of the body is pulled and pushed against this anchorage as the worm moves forwards.

Snails and slugs have a single foot covered with slimy mucus, which works in a similar fashion. The front of the foot anchors it to the ground, while the rest is contracted forwards. The rear of the foot then forms the anchor, while the front portion is extended forwards. The mucus helps the process.

Segment about to elongate and push head forwards

Segments move forward while elongated

Segment about to contract and pull tail forwards

Segments stationary and anchored while contracted

Liquid mucus
Solid mucus
Extended
Contracted

► Millipedes are specially adapted for burrowing. Their many legs enable them to push through loose soil with great force. Centipedes and millipedes hold all the records for numbers of legs. Centipedes have a single pair of legs on each segment of the body. In some species, like the common house centipede, the legs are quite long and well developed. Millipedes have two pairs of legs on each segment. A millipede's body may have nearly 200 segments, and 600-legged millipedes are common.

Movement in air

Only three kinds of living animal have mastered the art of flying: insects, birds and bats. All three have evolved completely different wing structures to move them through the air.

An insect's wings are shaped by a network of thin tubes that are pumped full of liquid to keep them rigid. Not all insects have wings, but those that do use either one or two pairs for flying.

In birds, the entire front limb has evolved into a wing. The bones are hollow and filled with air to make them light, but they are still very strong. Feathers smooth out the shape of the wing, and provide insulation and delicate flight control.

Bats are the only flying mammals. The fingers of their "hand" have become greatly elongated. A tough, leathery skin covers the span of the fingers and stretches right back to the hindlegs. This forms the wing surface. A bat flies by using all four of its limbs.

Insects keep themselves aloft by beating their wings, sometimes as fast as hundreds of times every second. Birds and bats can fly with far slower movements because their wings are large enough to make use of air currents. However, the smallest birds usually have to flap their wings very fast. Most birds make use of their wing shape to provide additional lift. Some birds, such as gulls and birds of prey, spend most of their time gliding and soaring, and only need to flap their wings occasionally.

► The Sugar glider can glide for long distances through the air. It has developed a membrane of skin along the sides of the body. When the limbs are stretched out, it can glide from tree to tree. Flying fish can glide above the surface of the water using enlarged fins.

▼ A Blue tit in flight. The downstroke of the wings provides the power. Then, the flight feathers are closed flat. The feathers open on the upstroke, allowing the air to pass through more easily.

► Taking off and landing are the trickiest parts of flying for many flying animals, particularly insects. They have to hurl themselves into the air, and usually rely on very rapid wing-beats to keep them aloft.

Movement in water

Movement in water presents its own problems, because all organisms float, or are buoyant. Unless they anchor themselves to the bottom, they tend to rise to the surface. Movement in water is therefore largely a matter of controlling buoyancy. Fish and some other underwater animals have developed special organs, called swim bladders, for this purpose. All their muscle power can therefore be devoted to providing propulsion. They also have a streamlined shape, which allows them to move through water more easily.

Fish swim by flexing their bodies lengthways, pushing through the water with their vertical tails. The fins are normally used only to alter direction, but some fish use fin movements to swim very slowly. Most mammals, birds and adult amphibians have to use muscle power to fight the lifting effect of the water. They swim by using all four of their limbs. The mammals that live in water, such as seals and whales, have specially adapted limbs for swimming.

Many invertebrates have other means of propulsion. For example, squid jet-propel themselves through the water.

▼ Otters are superb swimmers. They can travel more than 400 m underwater without coming up for air. But they must constantly use up energy just to keep below the surface. Propulsion comes from the hindlegs, which have webbed feet. The tail is used only for steering.

◄ A leaping frog. Once they have changed from tadpoles into adults, frogs have to swim using their limbs. In many frogs, the hindlegs are elongated and have very powerful muscles. These are equally useful for swimming or jumping. Not all frogs have webbed feet. Those that live on land are quite poor swimmers.

▼ Angel fish. All fish have a streamlined shape, and some have a very narrow frontal profile. This reduces the drag of the water on the body and allows them to move more easily through the water. The narrowest profiles are found among fish that inhabit coral reefs, which are a maze of swirling currents. By turning to face the current, the fish can avoid being buffeted around.

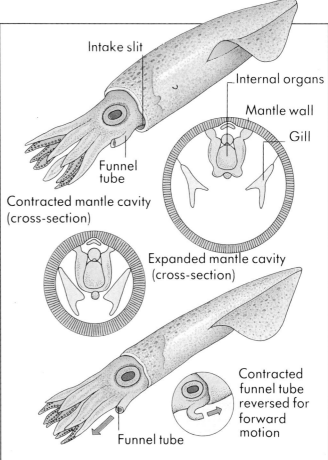

Intake slit

Internal organs

Mantle wall

Gill

Funnel tube

Contracted mantle cavity (cross-section)

Expanded mantle cavity (cross-section)

Contracted funnel tube reversed for forward motion

Funnel tube

Jet propulsion

Squid have developed a very effective means of movement – jet propulsion. When the body is relaxed, water can flow into the body cavity. When the muscles are contracted, the water is trapped and is forced out through a narrow tube. By relaxing and contracting the muscles rapidly, squid can reach speeds of 30-40 km/h.

◄ Dolphins, like whales, are mammals that have developed a fish-like appearance to suit their life in the sea. The hindlegs have disappeared entirely, and the forelimbs are reduced to mere paddles. Unlike fish, whales and dolphins swim by flexing their tails up and down. The horizontal flukes on the tail provide extra power. Dolphins can use their front flippers rather like the wings of a bird, only in reverse. By adjusting the angle of the flippers, dolphins can dive or surface rapidly with the minimum of additional effort.

Glossary

air sacs "Bags" leading off the lungs of birds, which make possible high rates of respiration.

algae A group of primitive plants, which includes single-celled plants and seaweeds.

amino acids A group of complex organic molecules that can link together to form proteins. They are considered to be the building blocks of life.

amphibians A group of vertebrates, which spend part of their lives in water, part on land. The young live in water and breathe through gills. The adults breathe air.

antennae Sense organs found on the heads of insects and some shellfish. Antennae are capable of "tasting" specific chemicals.

asexual reproduction Reproduction without sex, or the need for male and female cells to join together.

binary fission The process by which cells, and some primitive animals, reproduce by dividing into two identical halves.

blastosphere A stage in the development of a new individual from a fertilized egg; a hollow sphere that contains about 10,000 cells.

budding The way the hydra, for example, reproduces. It grows a "bud" on its body, which separates and becomes a new individual.

carbohydrate One of the basic categories of food that is easily converted into energy. Sugar and starch are both carbohydrates.

carpel The female part of a flower, which contains the ovary.

carnivore An animal that eats the meat of other animals.

cell The basic unit from which all living things are made up. A plant cell differs mainly from an animal cell by having a rigid cell wall.

cellulose A tough, fibrous type of carbohydrate that forms the outer wall of plant cells.

chlorophyll A green pigment contained by the chloroplasts of plant cells. When activated by sunlight, chlorophyll converts water and carbon dioxide into food.

chloroplast A unit in a plant cell that contains chlorophyll and takes part in photosynthesis.

chromosome One of a series of paired structures that carry a cell's DNA during normal cell division. Sex cells contain only single chromosomes.

cilia Tiny, hair-like growths on the bodies of simple organisms. By waving the cilia, the organisms can move.

cytoplasm A jelly-like substance found in the cells of living things.

digestion The process by which animals' food is progressively broken down and absorbed inside the body. Most animals have a basically tubular digestive system.

DNA Deoxyribonucleic acid. A very complex molecule present in the nucleus of all cells that contains all the coded information needed to make a complete organism.

egg A female sex cell, or germ cell, which develops into a new individual when fertilized.

embryo A stage in the development of a new individual from a fertilized egg, during which the organs develop.

environment All physical conditions, e.g. land surface (or type of water), climate, atmosphere and other life-forms, that form the normal surroundings for a particular species.

enzyme One of a group of chemicals produced by all living organisms, and which are mainly used for the digestion of food and the manufacture of proteins.

exoskeleton The hard outer covering that provides shape and support for insects and some other animals that do not have an internal skeleton.

fats Materials produced by plants and animals which represent a store of energy. They form a major part of the human diet.

fertilization The first stage of sexual reproduction, in which a male sperm cell joins with a female egg cell to produce a single cell that will develop into a new individual.

flagella Long hair-like growths carried by simple organisms, usually singly or in pairs. The organisms move by beating the flagella in a whip-like motion.

foetus The final stage in the development of a new mammal prior to birth. A foetus is fully formed, but is incapable of independent life.

gene One of the dark bands visible on a chromosome under a microscope. Individual genes are believed to be responsible for inherited characteristics, such as blue eyes.

gestation The time between the fertilization and birth of a mammal, during which the young develops inside the mother.

gill The breathing organ in a fish, with which it extracts dissolved oxygen from the water.

habitat Natural surroundings in which a particular plant or animal exists. The term is much more specific and localized than the environment.

insectivore An animal that eats insects; one kind of carnivore.

intestines Part of the digestive

system below the stomach where most of the absorbtion of food takes place, with waste matter passing out of the lower end.

invertebrate Any animal that does not have an internal skeleton centered on the backbone. Insects, spiders, worms and shellfish are all invertebrates.

larva A stage in the life cycle of fishes, amphibians and insects that comes after hatching, but before the fully adult form is achieved.

mammals A group of vertebrate animals, which give birth to live young. The young are suckled by the mother on milk produced by her mammary glands. The animals include monotremes, marsupials and the placental mammals.

marsupials Mammals that give birth to underdeveloped young, which mature in a pouch. Koalas and kangaroos are marsupials.

membrane A thin flexible "skin" that surrounds cells. Most of the organs of the body are also covered and lined with membranes.

metamorphosis A change in the structure and appearance of an animal during its life cycle. The term is usually applied to the transformation of a young insect or amphibian into the final adult form.

mitochondria The small areas inside each cell that use oxygen to convert food into energy.

monotremes A group of primitive mammals, represented by the echidnas and the platypus, which give birth to undeveloped young.

natural selection The process in evolution which determines which adaptations are preserved and which are allowed to die out. In general, natural selection favours the survival of the fittest.

neuron A type of nerve cell that carries messages. An electrical impulse passes down the neuron and is then transmitted across a connection known as a synapse.

nucleus A small dark area found in virtually all living cells. The nucleus normally stores the cell's DNA, and controls the operation of the various organelles inside the cell.

organelle The general term for any of the specialized internal structures of a cell e.g. mitochondria and vacuoles.

organic Relating to a living thing.

organism A living thing.

ovary The part of a plant or animal that produces and stores female egg cells before they are fertilized.

parasite Any organism that does not obtain its own food, but which attaches itself to another organism (externally or internally) and feeds off it.

pheromone A chemical substance produced by one organism that affects another. Female moths, for example, produce pheromones to attract a mate.

photosynthesis The process by which nearly all plants can use sunlight to turn water and carbon dioxide into food.

placenta The organ that develops inside female mammals during pregnancy and which enables the developing foetus to make use of the mother's blood supply.

pollen The powdery yellow dust produced by the male sex organs of a flower, the stamens, which contains the male sex cells.

pollination The process in the sexual reproduction of plants during which the male cells (in the form of pollen grains) enter the female part of the plant (the carpel).

prey An animal hunted for food by another (predator).

protein One of the basic types of food. There are many chemical types of protein which are used as a building material by cells.

protozoa The collective term for all microscopic, single-celled animals e.g. the amoeba.

reproduction The process by which an organism produces offspring.

respiration The process of breathing by which waste carbon dioxide is exchanged for fresh.

ruminant One of a group of herbiverous animals, e.g. cows and deer, that chew their food a second time after the first stage of digestion has taken place.

senses The means by which an animal learns about its environment. The main senses are sight, hearing, smell, taste and touch.

sexual reproduction Reproduction involving two parents, male and female. The joining together of the male and female sex cells brings about fertilization and the development of the offspring.

sperm The male sex cell.

stamens The male parts of a flower.

uterus The organ found in female mammals in which the embryo (and later the foetus) grow and develop prior to birth absorbing nourishment from the mother.

vacuole The hollow space inside a cell. In animal cells the vacuole is used to contain food or waste products; in plant cells it is used to store sugary sap.

vertebrate Any animal that has a backbone and internal skeleton. All the advanced animals, from fishes to apes, are vertebrates.

zygote The first stage in the development of a new individual. A fertilized cell that will later develop into an embryo.

Index

pollination 14, *14*, 23
pregnancy 18
protein *7, 9, 25*
protozoa 8

R

rabbit *18*
reproduction 12-19
respiration 27
retina 30
ruminants *23*

S

scent 33
sea anemones *13*
seed 14
senses 28-35
sexual reproduction 12, 14-19

sight 29-31
skin *6*
smooth muscle cells 10, *11*
snail *12*
snake *34, 36*
sperm 12, 15, 18, *19*
spider 30, 33
spiny ant eater *18*
spiracles 27
stamen 14
stigma 14
strawberry plant *13*
striated muscle cells 10
style 14
suckling 18
synapse 11

T

tissue 9
touch 33

U

umbilical cord 18
uterus 18

V

vacuole 7
vegetative propagation 13

W

whales 34
wings 40
womb 18

Z

zygote 17

Further Reading

The Living Planet by David Attenborough (Collins, 1984)
Egg: Nature's Miracle of Packaging by Richard Burton (Collins, 1987)
Plant Ecology by Jennifer Cochrane (Wayland, 1988)
Discovering Nature by Midas Dekker (Exley, 1988)
Animals and Where They Live by John Feltwell (Dorling Kindersley, 1988)
Living Things (Science Alive Series) by Robin Kerrod (Macdonald, 1987)
Mammal; Pond and River (Eyewitness Guides) by Steve Parker (Dorling Kindersley, 1989)
The Living World by Donald Silver (Kingfisher, 1986)

Picture Credits